MEASLES AND MUMPS

MEASLES AND MUMPS

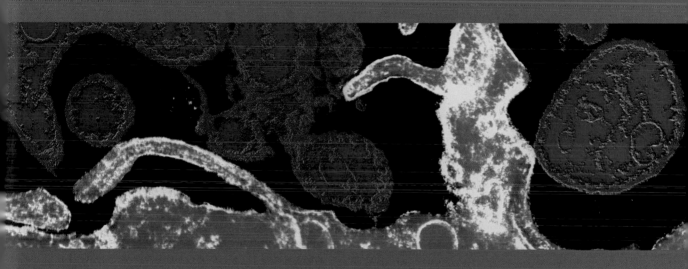

L. H. Colligan

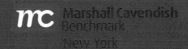

Marshall Cavendish
Benchmark
New York

With special thanks to Michael J. Smith, MD, MSCE, assistant professor of pediatrics at the University of Louisville School of Medicine, for his expert review of this manuscript.

Other Marshall Cavendish Offices:
Marshall Cavendish International (Asia) Private Limited, 1 New Industrial Road, Singapore 536196 • Marshall Cavendish International (Thailand) Co Ltd. 253 Asoke, 12th Flr, Sukhumvit 21 Road, Klongtoey Nua, Wattana, Bangkok 10110, Thailand • Marshall Cavendish (Malaysia) Sdn Bhd, Times Subang, Lot 46, Subang Hi-Tech Industrial Park, Batu Tiga, 40000 Shah Alam, Selangor Darul Ehsan, Malaysia

Marshall Cavendish is a trademark of Times Publishing Limited

All websites were available and accurate when this book was sent to press.

Library of Congress Cataloging-in-Publication Data

Colligan, L. H.
Measles and mumps / by L.H. Colligan.
p. cm. — (Health alert)
Summary: "Provides comprehensive information on the causes, treatment, and history of Measles and Mumps"—Provided by publisher.
Includes index.
ISBN 978-0-7614-4819-8
1. Measles—Juvenile literature. 2. Mumps—Juvenile literature. I. Title.
RC168.M4C65 2011
616.9'15--dc22

2009035556

Front Cover: A group of viruses that include the agents of human measles and mumps.
Title page: The measles virus.

Photo Research by Candlepants Incorporated
Cover Photo: Visuals Unlimited / Corbis

The photographs in this book are used by permission and through the courtesy of:
Photo Researchers Inc.: NIBSC, 3, 17; Biophoto Associates, 26; Saturn Stills, 44. *Getty Images*: Dr. Hans Gelderblom, 5, 14; Dr. Fred Hossler, 19; Lisa Spindler Photography Inc., 21; Peter Dazeley, 23, 47; Stock Montage, 35; Mark Kegans, 38; Jay Reilly, 45; Bernhard Lang, 51; Jose Luis Pelaez, 52. *Alamy Images*: imagebroker, 7; Hercules Robinson, 10; Mark Bourdillon, 41; Bubbles Photolibrary, 42; Medical-on-Line, 49;. *Corbis*: William Radcliffe/Science Faction, 15; Lester V. Bergman, 29; Bettmann, 33. *AP Images*: 31. 100

Editor: Joy Bean
Publisher: Michelle Bisson
Art Director: Anahid Hamparian

Printed in Malaysia(T)
6 5 4 3 2 1

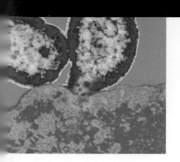

CONTENTS

1

WHAT IS IT LIKE TO HAVE MEASLES OR MUMPS?

Sarah remembers a couple things about catching **measles** back in fourth grade. One was being stuck in her room with the shades down for nearly two weeks. Her eyes hurt so much that she could not stand any light in the room. She also remembers having to stay in her room, away from her baby brother, so he would not get sick, too. But two-year-old Robbie caught the **infection** anyway. What Sarah remembers most was that her brother almost died after getting measles.

When Sarah got measles, she had already learned about the infection from her school nurse after a measles **outbreak** at school. The nurse had told students that they could catch the measles **virus** if they touched an infected person or breathed in that person's germs. She had said that measles germs are

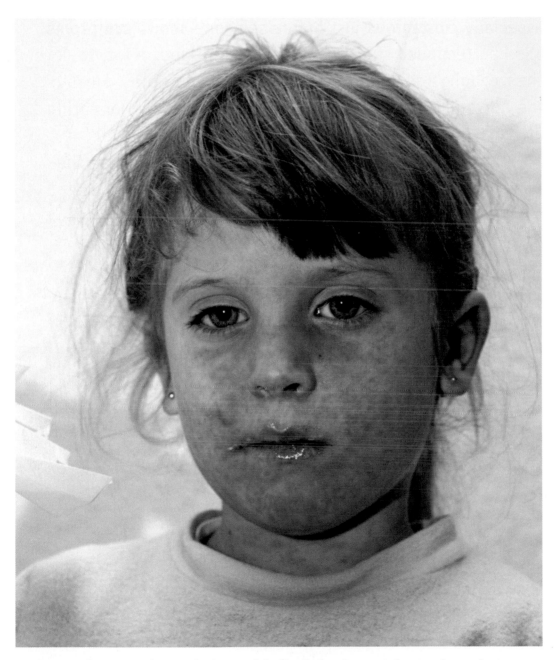

Having measles can make you feel very sick. Headache, fever, and eye pain are just some of the symptoms.

especially **contagious** just before someone shows **symptoms**. She had reminded students to wash their hands a lot, to cover their coughs and to use tissues to blow their noses. Finally, the nurse had told them not to share food, drinks, or eating utensils.

That advice was too late for Sarah. She soon had all the symptoms of measles—a bad headache, a high fever, eye pain with sensitivity to light, coughing fits, and a runny nose. She went through a few boxes of tissues while she was sick. Itchy measles spots soon followed, first on her head and then all over her body. After two weeks, all her symptoms went away.

Things were different for little Robbie. Because he was younger, Robbie got much sicker than Sarah did. He developed a serious lung infection called **pneumonia**. Sarah remembers overhearing her parents' worried voices. They spoke about some childhood friends who had died from brain and lung infections after getting the measles. It seemed impossible for that to happen to Robbie. He was such a tough little guy.

Sarah's parents took Robbie to the hospital as soon as he developed breathing problems. After a couple scary days, his pneumonia started to clear up. Robbie grew up to be one of those kids who never seemed to get sick. Later in life, he did not remember his close call with measles, but Sarah and the rest of her family never forgot it.

WHAT IS IT LIKE TO HAVE MUMPS?

Samantha Nolan is an adult. But no matter how many years pass, she will always remember the summer when she was ten. That was the year she lost most of her hearing in her left ear.

The problem started one summer during Samantha's stay at her sleepaway camp. One morning, two counselors did not show up at breakfast. The director told the campers that the counselors had come down with an infection called **mumps**. The sick counselors were already **quarantined**, or separated, from everyone else at camp. To be on the safe side, the camp was sending all the campers home for three weeks.

The campers could not believe the terrible news. The director explained that mumps is an infection that can be caught very easily. Fortunately, mumps usually does not cause permanent problems. People with mumps might get a fever, stomach pains, a sore throat, ear pain and feel tired. Their cheeks might swell up. Only a very small number of people develop serious **complications**. For example, some people lose their hearing from ear infections brought on by mumps.

The campers had a lot of questions. Could you catch mumps if you drank out of someone else's cup or shared forks and spoons? The answer was yes.

Within two days of getting home, Samantha developed severe mumps symptoms. She still remembers how awful she felt—as if she had two meatballs stuck in her throat. She could

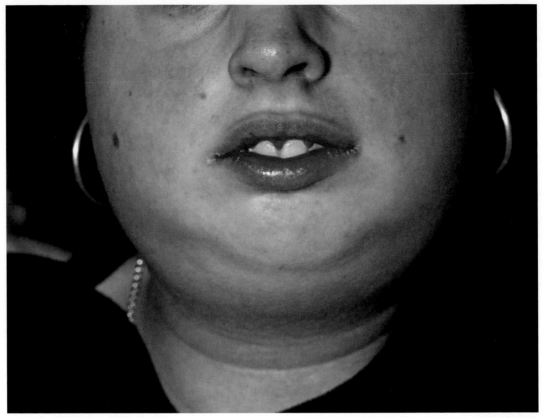

Having mumps means areas around your face and neck may get swollen.

feel two big, hard lumps between her ears and her jaw. She tried hard not to swallow because it hurt so much. Her right cheek was much more swollen than her left. Samantha's right ear also hurt. It felt as if someone had stuffed cotton in it.

Her parents became so worried that they took Samantha to the doctor's office for a hearing test. The results were upsetting. The mumps had caused an infection that had severely damaged Samantha's inner ear on the right side. Samantha remembers how scared she was when her parents said the hearing loss would be permanent. The doctor sent Samantha to a specialist who fitted her for a hearing aid. It was not perfect, but Samantha could hear better.

In the years to come, Samantha got married and had children of her own. New **vaccine** shots were available to protect children from mumps and other childhood infections. Since Samantha had firsthand experience with mumps, she and her husband decided to vaccinate their children. Although long-term problems such as Samantha's partial deafness are rare, she did not want to take any chances.

2

WHAT ARE MEASLES AND MUMPS?

Measles and mumps are two separate, easy-to-catch **viral** infections that mainly affect children. Many people who are now over the age of fifty had measles or mumps when they were young. Some remember being covered with pink measles spots and feeling miserable for a couple of weeks or so. Those who got mumps remember how their cheeks swelled up like a squirrel's and how they could hardly swallow because of the pain.

But measles and mumps are not completely infections of the past. Large outbreaks still happen in parts of the world where public health services are limited. In most countries, though, measles and mumps are pretty rare. In the 1960s, scientists developed vaccines that almost always protect people from getting measles or mumps. Before vaccination programs, large outbreaks meant that large numbers of children, and some adults, developed complications from measles or mumps. Widespread measles outbreaks caused many cases of blindness and millions of deaths from brain infections and pneumonia. Mumps once caused many cases of deafness and other permanent problems.

VIRUSES

It is hard to believe that so many people—mainly babies and children—can catch measles or mumps from something incredibly small. Viruses are tiny chemical particles. They can attack any living organism, including humans. In fact, viruses *must* invade living organisms in order to survive. They are not actually alive by themselves. They are **parasites** that do not reproduce on their own. They can only multiply when they take over the **cells** of a live **host**—such as us! When an invaded cell reproduces, so does the virus.

Like viruses, cells are also tiny packets of chemicals. They make up all the living parts of our bodies. Unlike viruses, cells are alive. They do reproduce on their own. Inside each cell are chemical instructions that tell different parts of the body what to do. When a virus invades a cell, the virus tells the cell what to do instead: "Copy me." Soon the virus is in charge of the cell. It becomes alive and begins to reproduce. When that happens, the workings of the body can go very wrong. The host gets sick.

Most scientists agree that measles and mumps viruses

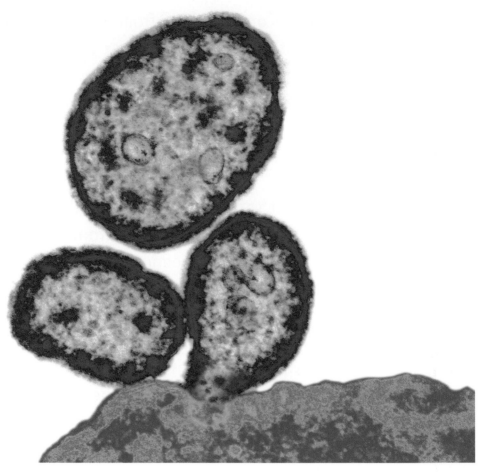

This measles virus, magnified 100,000 times, is multiplying.

probably reach the cells of human hosts by traveling in air-
borne droplets. Measles or mumps droplets get into the
air and on surfaces when an infected person breathes out,
talks, coughs, or sneezes. Direct contact—such as kissing or
sharing food, beverages, cups, or utensils—also spreads the
virus. Measles and mumps viruses hang out on drinking glasses,

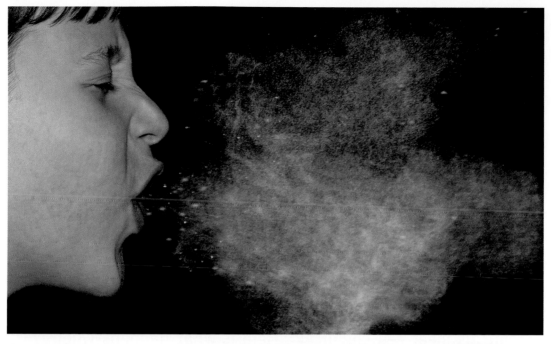

An uncovered sneeze or cough can travel great distances. Seen here, several thousand bacteria-laden droplets of mucus and saliva are in the air.

bottles, doorknobs, handrails, telephones, and other objects that happen to be nearby when infected people cough, sneeze, or touch things. That is why adults are always saying, "Wash your hands." "Use a tissue." "Cover your mouth when you cough." "Don't touch your nose, mouth, or eyes with your fingers."

Measles and mumps viruses are sneaky. They invade a person's cells without making the host sick right away. That means an infected person keeps doing everyday things—being near other people, playing, going to school or work, hugging, kissing, and so on—without feeling ill. But with every spoken word, sneeze, cough, or kiss, an infected host spreads the virus to others.

Measles and mumps are not only sneaky but also highly contagious. In groups of people who have not been vaccinated or had the measles virus before, about 95 percent get measles when they are exposed to someone with the infection. Mumps is highly contagious as well, though outbreaks do not happen as often as measles outbreaks do.

Measles and Mumps Chemistry

Viruses, and the cells they invade, are made up of chemicals, mainly **proteins**. A chemical reaction takes place when viral chemicals meet cell chemicals. Here is what happens when they meet:

- Protein chemicals in measles or mumps viruses try to attach to the tough protein coating of certain cells inside a host's nose, mouth, or eyes. An attachment forms when the viruses find certain chemical cell **receptors** that "fit." If someone has had measles or mumps before, or has been vaccinated against the infections, the virus cannot lock on to the cell. It does not fit. In an unprotected person, the virus does fit.
- After a successful attachment, the measles or mumps virus injects strands of its own chemical instructions into

a cell. Infected cells turn into measles-or mumps-copying factories.

- Each infected cell fills up with the virus. New viruses burst out of the cells, form new attachments, and inject themselves into nearby cells. The whole body becomes infected even before the host feels sick.

The chemistry of viral infections works pretty well for viruses. Fortunately, the human body has a natural defense system to deal with harmful invaders.

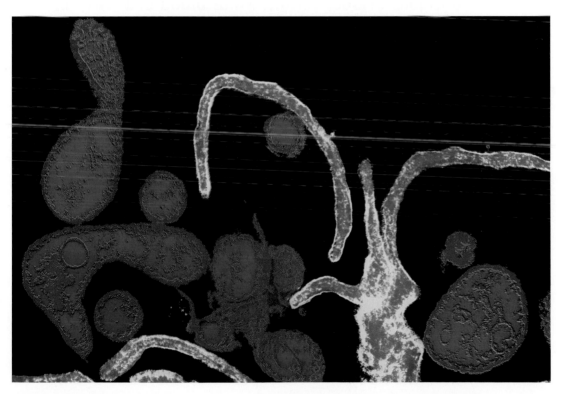

The measles virus (in red) is attacking and infecting a cell (in yellow and pink).

THE IMMUNE SYSTEM

Harmful germs, such as **bacteria** and viruses, are all around us, yet most people are healthy most of the time. Why is that? A healthy **immune system** is the body's first line of defense. It is always on the lookout for invaders that might make us sick. Certain **white blood cells** watch out for attackers that do not belong in the body. These attackers may be poisons, bacteria, or viruses, such as measles or mumps. The parts of the attackers that white blood cells recognize are called **antigens**.

When antigens invade, certain white blood cells rush to them. They produce protein **antibodies** that recognize, mark, and remember those antigens. Then the immune system plays offense. It sends out other white blood cells to destroy the marked antigens.

Once the fight is over, some white blood memory cells stay in the immune system. If a similar invader appears in the future, these memory cells recognize and fight it off again. This is why people get sick only once from certain viruses, such as measles or mumps. It is also the reason that vaccines work so well. Vaccines contain parts of viruses or bacteria. In some cases they contain live viruses that have been weakened. These vaccines usually do not make someone sick, but they are enough to get the immune system to produce antibodies. Later on, if a vaccinated person gets exposed to the virus again, antibodies remember that type of antigen and fight it off.

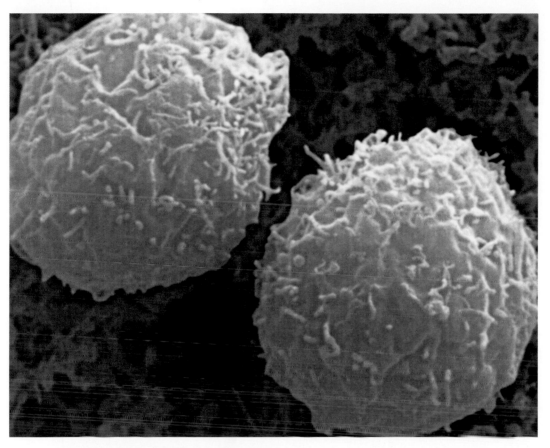

White blood cells fight invaders in the body.

If immune systems could fight off all harmful antigens, people would never get sick. However, some invading antigens, such as those inside measles or mumps viruses, are powerful enough to knock out white blood cells. When the immune system is down, other infections can invade the body.

Some people have immature or weak immune systems to begin with. Infants are born with protection from their

Following the Herd

. . . .

Imagine a classroom with twenty students. Eighteen of them either had measles in the past or received the measles vaccine. That means certain white blood cells in their immune systems can recognize and then attack the measles virus. The two remaining students do not have measles antibodies. They have had neither the infection nor the vaccine. Now imagine that another student joins the class. He has just returned from a country where there was a measles outbreak. He carries the measles virus into the classroom but does not know it yet. How many of the twenty students will catch measles?

Perhaps none! The two unprotected students may escape the disease thanks to the other eighteen. That large group may protect the others due to their **herd immunity**. Here is how that works. In order to reproduce, all viruses need a chain of hosts to infect one another by sneezing, coughing, or sharing germs in some way. In our imaginary classroom, however, protected students— the "herd"—outnumber the two unprotected ones. The virus does not have enough hosts to pass along the infection. The odds are eighteen to two against the virus.

Beginning in the late 1980s, a number of measles and mumps outbreaks occurred in the United States and in other countries. That happened because the herd of immune individuals was too small to protect greater numbers of unvaccinated children and young adults.

mothers' immune systems and get an additional boost from breastfeeding. However, babies lose some of that immunity before they are a year old. Elderly people also have weakened immune systems. Certain medical conditions, such as allergies, diabetes, and AIDS, can also weaken the immune system. Unvaccinated people who have caretakers with weak immune systems should check with a doctor about whether they should get vaccinated, since caretakers are at a high risk for developing measles or mumps complications.

Infants have weakened immune systems because they have not been alive long enough to develop immunity to some bacteria and viruses.

MEASLES

The measles virus is also called rubeola. People may be infected with rubeola for up to two weeks before symptoms appear. They will not feel sick during that **incubation period**. They become contagious to others a few days before symptoms appear and stay contagious until after the symptoms disappear about two weeks later. If unvaccinated adults catch measles, they often develop more severe symptoms than unvaccinated children do.

Measles Symptoms

- A fever between 100 and 104 degrees Fahrenheit (38 and 40 degrees Celsius) that lasts about three to four days. The fever is a sign that the immune system is heating up the body to kill off the virus.
- Heavy coughing and a runny nose.
- Runny, red eyes from an infection called **conjunctivitis**. The person's eyes are extremely sensitive to light at this time.
- White **Koplik's spots** in the mouth.
- A red rash, which later becomes brown, that starts on the head and moves down the body. The rash is a sign that blood vessels are reacting to the foreign antigens in the bloodstream.
- Vomiting and diarrhea that sometimes occur as the body tries to rid itself of the measles virus.

Anyone with measles symptoms should be kept away from unvaccinated people until all symptoms disappear.

Complications

Measles complications are rare. That is because measles outbreaks are rare in countries with healthy, well-fed populations and large groups of vaccinated children. Complications are more common in people who are underfed or already sick, although anyone may be affected. A weakened immune system gives certain infections an opportunity to cause pneumonia, measles-

One of the symptoms of measles is a runny nose combined with a heavy cough.

related **encephalitis**, blindness, deafness, or dehydration from uncontrollable diarrhea and vomiting.

Pregnant women who get measles early in the pregnancy have an increased risk of miscarriage—losing their unborn

German Measles

A milder kind of measles, caused by the *rubella* virus, also spreads among people in close contact. **German measles** victims are mainly unvaccinated children who develop a low fever, cold symptoms, and possibly a rash. Rubella is sometimes called three-day measles because its symptoms usually last just a few days.

However, there may be serious consequences for the fetuses of unvaccinated women who catch German measles during the first five months of pregnancy. A rubella-infected baby may be born blind, deaf, or with heart problems. One out of ten babies born with rubella dies during the first twelve months of life.

To prevent German measles, doctors strongly advise unvaccinated women to get the German measles vaccine before they get pregnant. Doctors do not vaccinate pregnant women because the small amount of virus in the vaccine may infect the fetus. Pregnant woman who do not know whether they ever had the vaccination, or the virus, can get a simple blood test to find out.

fetus. If measles occurs late in the pregnancy, the mother's baby may not be born alive.

About two of every thousand people—mainly those under the age of five—who get measles will die of complications. The World Health Organization (WHO) reported that around the world, measles deaths—mostly in African countries—fell from about 750,000 in the year 2000 to 197,000 in 2007. About 90 percent of the deaths were children under five years old. This significant decrease in global measles death rates is due to improved living conditions and greatly increased vaccination rates.

MUMPS

Mumps is a viral infection of the **salivary glands**. These glands are located just under both sides of the jaw between the ears and chin. These small organs, which produce saliva (spit), are also called **parotid glands**. Mumps infections depend on direct contact with a host's saliva. The salivary glands swell up on one or both sides after the mumps virus attacks them. Swelling is a sign that white blood cells have sent antibodies to fight off the mumps virus. Uncomplicated mumps usually lasts around a week.

Symptoms

A mumps-infected host may carry the virus without any symptoms for more than two weeks. A host is most likely to infect someone else a few days before symptoms break out and until symptoms clear up. The main symptoms of uncomplicated mumps usually develop in the following way:

- Headaches, poor appetite, and tiredness are usually the first mumps symptoms to appear.
- Both chills and high fevers are possible, as the immune system causes muscles to shiver in order to overheat the body and kill off the virus.
- Swallowing starts to become difficult.
- Salivary glands on one or both cheeks swell up within a day or two of the earlier symptoms. The swelling is worst the first two or three days.

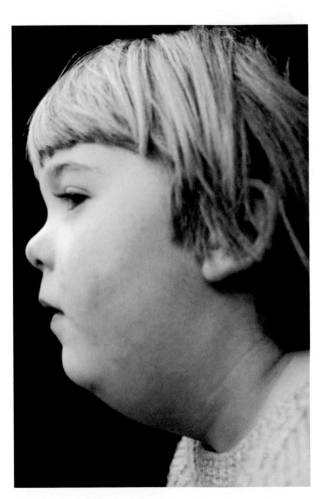

The parotid gland becomes swollen in people who have mumps.

- Other glands near the ear and throat areas usually swell up, too.
- The swollen glands cause severe pain during swallowing and chewing.

Someone who has had the mumps will not get the infection again. However, in some cases, a vaccinated person may catch the infection if he or she did not receive an effective vaccination.

Complications

As with measles, infants, adults, the elderly, and those who are underfed or sick with something else are at risk for mumps complications. These may include mumps-related **meningitis**, mumps-related encephalitis, damage to the inner ear, and infections of other organs. **Orchitis**, an infection of the male sex organs, can affect teens and young adults.

Researchers now know a lot about measles and mumps. Government groups, such as the Centers for Disease Control and Prevention (CDC), watch for outbreaks. They alert the public so that parents can watch out for these infections. Both measles and mumps are rare in healthy, well-fed populations with good immunization programs.

3

THE HISTORY OF MEASLES AND MUMPS

Measles and mumps have been around for thousands of years. Preventive vaccines against these two infections have been around for less than sixty years. In that short time, immunization has been so successful that most children's doctors have never seen anyone with these infections. But this was not always the case.

THE HISTORY OF MEASLES

Scientists are still trying to figure out how certain human viruses began. Measles probably developed thousands of years ago when people began to raise animals and live near them. The measles virus has a similar structure to a cattle virus called rinderpest. That virus may have jumped from cattle to humans by changing form slightly. To succeed, these human and cattle viruses needed large groups of hosts to infect.

For thousands of years, people did not live in large crowds. Instead, small groups of people hunted animals and gathered plants to eat. That way of living began to change around ten thousand years ago. People began to grow crops on farms and to raise animals instead of hunt them. They began to settle in farming villages and cities in what is now the Middle East. Large, close groups of human hosts made it

Measles and mumps are rare now, but just a few decades ago, children with measles were quarantined so they would not infect other children.

possible for certain animal and human viruses to multiply.

As populations grew, deadly measles **epidemics** spread throughout the Middle East, Asia, and Europe. Up until the 1960s, measles was so common that nearly all children caught the infection. Getting measles seemed to be a normal part of growing up, even though its complications killed millions of people.

Timeline of Measles Breakthroughs

. . . .

- 850–923 C.E.: A Persian doctor named Muhammad ibn Zakariya ar-Razi first identifies the illness we know as measles.
- 1754: A doctor named Francis Home deliberately injects the blood of a measles-infected child into several other children. The other children come down with measles, proving that humans catch the infection from one another.
- 1840s: During a measles outbreak, a medical officer, Peter Panum, visits the faraway Faroe Islands in Denmark. He notes that no one over the age of sixty-five became infected. Panum figures out that the older people must have gotten immunity during a previous measles outbreak when they were children.
- 1954: Two doctors in the United States, John Enders and Thomas Peebles, identify and grow the measles virus in a laboratory. Isolating the virus lays the foundation for later researchers. Enders and Peebles figure out that growing and injecting weakened forms of the measles virus might be a way to get the immune system to make antibodies against the measles virus.
- 1963: Widespread vaccination begins after Dr. Maurice Hilleman and other scientists succeed in producing the measles vaccine by growing the virus inside millions of fertilized eggs.

- 2001: The American Red Cross, the World Health Organization (WHO), and other leading public health groups launch the Measles Initiative. Its purpose is to reduce worldwide measles deaths by 90 percent by 2010. By 2007, the worldwide death rate from measles since 2000 had plunged by 74 percent.

- Today, every state in the United States has public school laws requiring entering students to be vaccinated. However, parents can request that their children not be immunized due to religious or certain medical reasons.

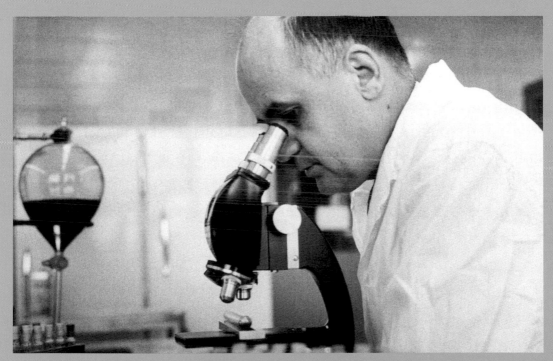

Dr. Maurice Hilleman at work studying viruses.

On the other side of the world, in the Western Hemisphere, measles arrived late. In the New World, many natives still lived as hunter-gatherers until the late 1400s. Others lived in small cities and villages. They raised few animals from which a virus might have jumped to humans. These New World natives had other illnesses, but they did not have measles or mumps.

In 1492, that changed. After Christopher Columbus arrived in the New World, waves of other European explorers soon followed. The earliest explorers found healthy, active natives living in small settlements or hunting and gathering. Later explorers found deserted villages and sick, weak natives.

What happened in between? Explorer groups had arrived in the New World without realizing that some of them carried dangerous infections, including smallpox, measles, and mumps. These infections proved to be deadlier than weapons. With no protective antibodies whatsoever, the great majority of New World natives caught the new infections. Millions died from them in agony. Historians have estimated that the native population in what is now Mexico dropped from 25 million to 3 million people between 1500 and the early 1600s. No wonder later explorers found a sickly, depressed native population that struggled to survive.

Measles, along with other deadly infections, changed the course of history. Surviving native people were too sick to defend themselves. Their large populations collapsed. That

When explorers arrived in the New World, they brought their diseases with them.

made it easier for immigrants to settle in the New World. With increased settlement, measles had the huge populations it needed to reproduce in the Western Hemisphere. Wherever the new immigrants traveled, so did measles. Measles became as common in the New World as it had been in the Old World— and it stayed that way right up to the middle of the twentieth century.

Here is how one children's doctor, Kenneth D. Moss, described a measles outbreak that sent many children to his hospital in the days before mass vaccinations began:

By 1963, I was a resident at the Cincinnati [Ohio] Children's and General Hospital where I spent a lot of time in the emergency wards and receiving wards. As house staff physicians, we saw hundreds of cases of the last big measles epidemic that was sweeping the country. Again, it was not a mild illness at all. A large proportion of the children had . . . pneumonia. Many had . . . ear infections. . . . All of them had raging headaches, [sensitivity to light], listlessness, dehydration, and lethargy. Lots of penicillin shots were given to try to keep kids out of hospital beds, but sometimes they wound up there simply because they were so sick they could not be cared for at home.

One day I was on the neurological ward at the Children's Hospital and saw a very handsome lad of about ten years old. He was sitting in a large crib and rocking back and forth, staring vacantly, and moaning. When I reviewed his chart, it revealed that he'd suffered the measles complication of encephalitis. This is unusual—one in one thousand cases incidence—but for this boy it meant he was left in a nonverbal, blind state from damage to his nervous system from the measles virus.

Public health immunization in most advanced countries put an end to most of these heartbreaking scenes. Measles became controllable in most of the world.

Recent Measles Outbreaks

In the spring of 2008, eight brothers and sisters in a Washington State family came down with measles. Three of the siblings were hospitalized with pneumonia. They were part of a measles outbreak of 131 cases that the CDC reported from January to July 2008. Ninety percent of the infected children had not been vaccinated or their vaccination status was unknown. Four infants were among the fifteen patients hospitalized with measles complications.

The History of Mumps

Like measles, mumps is an old infection that affected historical events. During the largest mumps epidemic ever, more soldiers in World War I were hospitalized with mumps than with war injuries. But mumps outbreaks go back much farther than that. The first known mention of mumps appeared more than 2,500 years ago. That is when the famous Greek physician Hippocrates (460–370 B.C.E.), wrote about mumps:

An illustration of Hippocrates from 400 B.C.E.

35

Swellings appeared about the ears, in many on either side, and in the greatest number on both sides. . . .They seized children, adults, and mostly those who were engaged in the exercises of the . . . gymnasium, but seldom attacked women. Many had dry coughs without expectoration [phlegm], and accompanied with hoarseness of voice. In some instances earlier, and in others later, inflammations with pain seized sometimes one of the testicles, and sometimes both; some of these cases were accompanied with fever and some not; the greatest part of these were attended with much suffering. In other respects they were free of disease, so as not to require medical assistance.

This is pretty much what doctors say about mumps today. The one exception is that females also get mumps. Back in Hippocrates's day, girls lived more sheltered lives than boys. They were less likely than boys to be involved in public activities where they might catch mumps infections that were going around.

Like measles, mumps is now rare in developed countries with good vaccination coverage. Mumps rates are dropping fast, even in countries that once had many cases.

Recent Mumps Outbreaks
Nowadays mumps viruses usually arrive in North America when unvaccinated hosts travel from a foreign country experiencing

Timeline of Mumps Breakthroughs

. . . .

- 400 B.C.E.: The Greek doctor Hippocrates describes mumps in his book *Of Epidemics*.
- Sixteenth century: Guillaume de Baillou records a mumps epidemic in Paris, France, but no further studies are done.
- 1790: British physician Robert Hamilton (1721–1793) writes a scientific account of his experience of treating mumps-infected soldiers.
- 1921: Martha Wollstein, an American doctor, produces mumps like symptoms in cats by injecting them with saliva from a mumps patient.
- 1934: Claude D. Johnson and Ernest William Goodpasture (1886–1960), two American researchers, prove that mumps is a virus. This lays the foundation for growing and developing live vaccines.
- 1948: Dr. John Enders does the groundwork for developing a live mumps vaccine.

large mumps outbreaks. One outbreak happened at a summer camp in New York State in 2005. It is thought that an unvaccinated counselor from the United Kingdom arrived at the camp while carrying the mumps virus.

The largest U.S. mumps outbreak in twenty years—more than a thousand cases—happened in 2006. It began in college dormitories in the Midwest. Eighty-five young people were hospitalized with mumps complications. This was worrisome to public health officials. Mumps can cause fertility problems

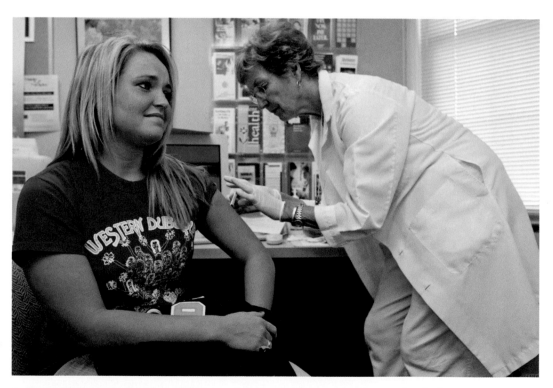

A student at the University of Iowa receives a mumps, measles, and rubella vaccination shot during the mumps outbreak in the Midwest in 2006.

in teenage and young adult males who get the infection in both testicles. They may become infertile.

What makes the recent mumps outbreaks different from measles outbreaks is that some of the victims in the 2005 and 2006 outbreaks had received at least part of their mumps vaccinations. Researchers are exploring whether the mumps vaccines were too weak or the virus strain was somehow different. Still, vaccination coverage was high. More than 90 percent of vaccinated campers, as well as the college students, did not get sick if they had had the two recommended mumps shots.

Like measles, the mumps infection, which once affected millions of people, has become manageable. In modern times, in most countries, the "herds" of immunized children keep measles and mumps in check. The viruses have fewer places to reproduce.

4

PREVENTING, DIAGNOSING, AND TREATING MEASLES AND MUMPS

In 2006, and then in 2008, the CDC reported something that it had not reported for a long time. Measles and mumps cases increased. These outbreaks put children's doctors and public health officials on the alert. They reminded the public of the importance of preventing these two infections.

When outbreaks of measles or mumps begin, public health officials act quickly. Bulletins go out to hospitals, doctors, websites, newspapers, and radio and television stations. These alerts describe the symptoms people may have. They also advise parents to keep their children home if they suspect measles or mumps, unless complications develop and a doctor's visit becomes necessary. Such efforts have helped to contain several outbreaks.

PREVENTING MEASLES AND MUMPS

Although vaccines prevent deaths and complications from measles and mumps, some parents worry about immunizing their children. They may belong to religions that forbid medical procedures, for example. Other parents decide not to vaccinate their children because they know that herd immunity will likely protect their own children. These parents also realize that most healthy, well-fed children are unlikely to develop complications if they do get either measles or mumps.

Some parents delay immunizing their babies until they are older. They believe the immune systems of children will better be able to deal with possible reactions to the vaccine, although this has never been proven. This strategy can be risky. Babies

Some parents of young children worry about getting them immunized.

are more frequently hospitalized with measles or mumps complications than older children are.

Occasionally some parents expose their children to measles or mumps on purpose if the infections are going around and their children are otherwise healthy. That is what many parents did in the days before vaccination. The military also used this strategy during wartimes in order to contain measles and mumps outbreaks off the battlefield. However, most doctors do not advise this.

Some parents are concerned that the combined measles, mumps, and rubella (MMR) vaccine shots are harmful. The shots sometimes produce temporary side effects, such as a low fever, a rash, and tiredness. A very small number of children—one in a million—have an allergic reaction to the MMR shot. When this happens, the child may experience **seizures**, which are temporary brain and muscle disturbances.

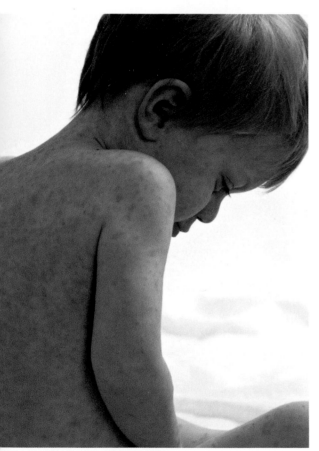

Children who are not immunized are susceptible to getting measles, like this toddler, or mumps.

Some parents avoid vaccinating their children because they are worried about a permanent brain disorder called **autism.** This trend began after 1998 when one doctor's study of twelve autistic children in England seemed to show a relationship between the MMR vaccine and autism. Researchers who have run much larger studies since that time have not been able to repeat this research with the same results. Large, recent, well-designed studies have shown no connection whatsoever between the MMR vaccine and autism.

The February 15, 2009, issue of *Clinical and Infectious Diseases* reports that Dr. Paul Offit and co-author Dr. Jeffrey Gerber, also of the Children's Hospital of Philadelphia, reviewed more than a dozen large studies using different methods to address the issue. They concluded that no data supported the association between the MMR vaccine and autism. The connection is merely coincidental, the authors say, because the MMR vaccine is given at the age when autism symptoms usually appear.

Immunization is important for young men and women. Young adults who are temporarily sick with something else are at risk of measles or mumps complications while their immune systems are busy fighting off the other illness. Unvaccinated women run the danger of catching these infections when they are pregnant. That puts their unborn babies at risk. Mumps can affect the fertility of young men who develop orchitis.

Measles, Mumps, and Rubella Vaccination Schedule

· ·

The CDC recommends the following MMR vaccination schedule for babies and children:

- The first MMR shot should be given to babies between twelve and fifteen months of age. However, if there is a local outbreak of measles or mumps, the shot can be given earlier.

- The second shot is usually given to children before they enter kindergarten, but it can be given as early as a month after the first shot. The second shot is meant to immunize most of the 20 percent of children who did not get fully immunized after the first shot.

- An MMR shot given within seventy-two hours to an unvaccinated person exposed to someone with measles can prevent the infection.

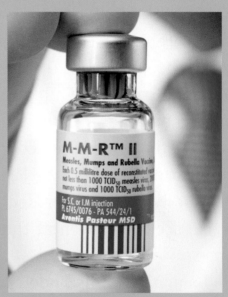

One dose of the MMR vaccine.

People with severely weakened immune systems, such as those with tuberculosis, leukemia, cancer, or AIDS, should not get MMR shots, but their caregivers should. Pregnant women should not get the MMR shot. The parents of severely allergic children should discuss vaccinations with their doctors. It was once thought that children allergic to eggs should not get the shot. However, many recent studies have disproved this.

It is recommended that pregnant woman do not get the MMR vaccination.

In addition, anyone who gets measles or mumps is a risk to unvaccinated babies, sick children, and adults with weakened immune systems.

Immunization rates remain high. A record number of toddlers in the United States received their vaccinations in 2007. The protected herd is still large. These shots, which take only seconds, prevented millions of those toddlers from going through weeks of misery or suffering possible complications.

Staying Healthy

Here is the bad news about measles and mumps. Most unvaccinated children and adults exposed to someone with either infection will get it even if they have strong immune systems. The good news is that most healthy, well-fed children who catch measles or mumps will recover completely after a week or two of feeling miserable. Almost everyone recovers without complications if he or she is healthy to begin with. It is very rare that someone who has had measles or mumps gets the disease again.

The best way to get healthy and to stay that way is to have healthy habits. Eat a diet that includes lots of fruits, vegetables, and whole grains. Get protein from beans, soy, fish, eggs, milk, lean meats, and poultry. A strong body helps the immune system fight invaders, so exercise is an important part of staying healthy. A healthy heart, liver, kidneys, and

Keeping healthy is an everyday process. Eating a healthy meal three times a day helps keep the body healthy.

other organs make it possible for immune system cells to get around and to do their jobs in controlling infections. Good sleep habits are important, too. During sleep, certain organs release chemicals that build up the immune system. Children and teens need eight to ten hours of sleep a night.

Vaccinated or not, everyone should avoid sharing others' drinking cups, water bottles, eating utensils, food, and drinks. Washing hands and covering coughs and sneezes can help control viruses. If unvaccinated people discover that they have been around someone with measles or mumps, they should pay attention to the earliest symptoms—high fever and a bad headache.

Diagnosing and Treating Uncomplicated Measles

Like many viral illnesses, measles starts out with a high fever, headache, runny nose, and deep coughing. But measles is likely in an unvaccinated adult, child, or baby if the eyes become very red and runny and spots appear a few days after the first symptoms. Spots usually show up first in the mouth and then around the head.

Measles cannot be stopped once it starts. It is important to pay close attention to all symptoms in case another infection develops. Someone with measles should be separated, or quarantined, from unvaccinated people until all symptoms clear up. To comfort someone with measles, the following can help:

- Keep sick people in a dim, cool room so that light does not hurt their eyes.
- Make sure the sick person drinks plenty of fluids and easy-to-digest food. Ginger ale, seltzer, chopped ice, gelatin, and sherbet are good choices.

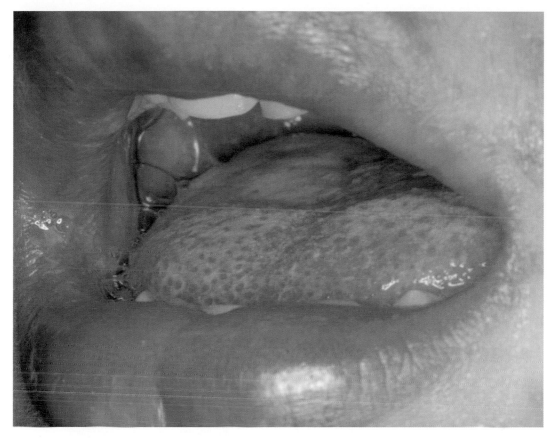

Koplik's spots are seen in this close-up image of a person with measles.

- Acetaminophen can relieve headache and fever discomfort. *Never give aspirin to people infected with measles.*
- Provide cool, wet cloths for aching eyes and an itchy rash.
- A cool mist vaporizer can help keep breathing passages unclogged.
- Provide plenty of tissues for runny noses. Dispose of them away from the family's other trash.

When to Call the Doctor

Call a doctor if someone gets measles and already has a different medical condition or is taking medication for it. Call a doctor immediately if any of the following symptoms develop: a fever above 105 °F (41 °C), gasping and breathing problems, seizures, severe diarrhea or vomiting, a sudden severe headache, a painful stiff neck, visual problems, mental confusion, and unresponsiveness. Call a doctor if any symptoms develop after the typical measles symptoms clear up, even weeks afterward. Here are some serious measles-related complications that require urgent medical attention:

- Bacterial or viral pneumonia. Both illnesses cause someone's lungs to fill up with fluid. The sick person has trouble breathing. Pneumonia brought on by measles can be deadly, especially in babies.
- Measles-related encephalitis. Sometimes the measles virus causes severe brain swelling, which may lead to permanent brain damage. About one in a thousand people who get measles develops encephalitis. Encephalitis symptoms may appear a few weeks after the measles rash disappears. A sudden high fever, severe headache, seizures, and unconsciousness are all signs of encephalitis. Anyone who gets such symptoms after seeming to recover from measles should get immediate medical attention.

If you develop a high fever, it could mean many things. A doctor should be called to find out what is wrong.

- Measles-related blindness. This can develop in underfed children. The children lack vitamin A in their diets due to poor nutrition.
- Uncontrollable diarrhea or vomiting. These symptoms may lead to dehydration and malnutrition, which are serious problems for children in countries with limited public health care.

Diagnosing and Treating Uncomplicated Mumps

Early mumps symptoms are vague—low energy, headache, chills, and lack of appetite. The main mumps symptoms follow

One way to check for mumps is for a doctor to feel for swollen glands under a person's jaw.

within a day or two. The salivary glands swell up under the jaw. Other glands in the throat, head, and neck swell up. The person gets a fever of around 104 °F (40 °C) and has great difficulty swallowing.

Because mumps is so rare, parents sometimes suspect other throat infections first. Mumps should be considered in an unvaccinated young adult, child, or baby if there has been a recent mumps outbreak. As with measles, pay close attention to symptoms in case other related infections develop. Keep the patient apart from unvaccinated people until all the symptoms clear up.

To make someone with mumps comfortable, these steps can help:

- Provide acetaminophen or ibuprofen—*never aspirin*—to relieve neck and throat pain.
- Offer cool water regularly to keep the person hydrated. Avoid citric juices, which cause swallowing pain. Dairy drinks and foods should be avoided since they are hard to digest.
- Offer soft foods such as sherbet, mashed potatoes, or even baby food as long as it is not acidic.

A mumps patient can go back to normal routines once all the symptoms have gone away.

When to Call the Doctor

Mumps symptoms usually clear up in a week or so. If they do not, or if symptoms such as headache and fever reappear, the patient should see a doctor right away. Call a doctor if an infant, an already sick child, or an adult gets mumps or is taking medications to treat another condition. Call a doctor immediately if any of the following symptoms develop: a fever above 105 °F (41 °C), gasping and breathing problems, seizures, severe diarrhea or vomiting, a sudden severe headache, a painful stiff neck, visual problems, mental confusion, or unresponsiveness. Call a doctor if any symptoms develop after the typical mumps symptoms clear up, even weeks afterward. Here are some serious mumps-related complications that require urgent medical attention:

- Mumps-related meningitis. This infection affects the fluids surrounding the brain and spinal cord in 15 percent of mumps cases. If meningitis develops, symptoms appear four or five days after earlier mumps symptoms. Mumps-related meningitis symptoms include a stiff neck, headache, vomiting, and tiredness. Although usually less dangerous and deadly than measles-related meningitis, mumps meningitis requires immediate medical attention. It generally clears up in a week or so.

- Mumps-related encephalitis. This can infect the brain, causing high fever, severe headache, and seizures, which cause temporary disturbances in the brain. Such encephalitis symptoms appear about two weeks after the first mumps symptoms. The death rate of mumps encephalitis is about one in a hundred.
- Orchitis. About one-quarter of male teenagers and male adults with mumps develop this painful swelling of the testicles. Symptoms of orchitis usually appear about a week after earlier symptoms. The teen or adult may experience severe pain in one or both testicles, as well as headache, fever, and nausea. There may be some shrinking of the testicles. Symptoms usually go away in a week or so.
- Mumps once caused permanent deafness—usually in one ear—in one in twenty thousand children. Due to mass vaccinations in developed countries, mumps is rare. That means mumps-related deafness is rare, too. But see a doctor if severe ear pain develops or does not go away.
- Very rare mumps complications may cause infections in organs such as the heart, pancreas, and kidneys. Researchers have noted that a condition called diabetes sometimes follows mumps outbreaks, but the relation-ship between diabetes and mumps is unknown.

Most parents and doctors will never have to treat measles or mumps in children. All over the world, rates of these once-deadly infections are dropping fast. The hope of all public health officials is that every country will be measles and mumps free.

GLOSSARY

antibodies—Proteins made by white blood cells that defend the body against tiny, disease-causing organisms.

antigens—Foreign substances that create an immune response.

autism—A mental disorder that causes abnormalities in a child's language development, behavior, and sense perceptions.

bacteria—One-celled organisms that reproduce by dividing.

cells—The smallest living units in organisms.

complications—Problems that may develop as a result of a medical condition.

conjunctivitis—A contagious eye infection that causes eyes to become red, runny, and itchy.

contagious—Easily passed from one person to another.

diagnosing—Identifying an illness by studying symptoms and running tests.

encephalitis—Inflammation of the brain, often due to viral infections.

epidemics—Widespread outbreaks of an infection.

German measles (rubella)—A mild, short-term viral infection similar to measles that can be harmful to the unborn babies whose mothers get it.

herd immunity—A type of immunity that occurs when the vaccination of a portion of the population provides protection to unprotected individuals.

host—A human or other organism in which another organism lives.

immune system—The body's system for fighting disease.

incubation period—The time period between exposure to an infection and the appearance of the first symptoms.

infection—An injury to the body caused by harmful germs such as certain bacteria and viruses.

Koplik's spots—Tiny white spots that may appear inside the mouth of a person who has measles.

measles (rubeola)—A contagious viral infection that produces a pink rash, among other symptoms.

meningitis—Inflammation of the fluids surrounding the brain and spinal cord, usually caused by viruses or bacteria.

mumps—A contagious viral infection that causes severe swelling of the salivary glands.

orchitis—An infection or inflammation of the testicles, which are male sex organs.

outbreak—The appearance of an infection among a group of people.

parasites—Organisms that must live on or within another organism in order to survive.

parotid glands—The glands under the jaw that produce saliva.

pneumonia—A serious lung infection caused by bacteria or viruses.

proteins—Chemical substances that serve as the basic building blocks for cells.

quarantined—Isolated in order to prevent an infection from passing to others.

receptors—Cells or groups of cells that receive stimuli.

salivary glands—Small organs under the jaw that produce saliva.

seizures—Temporary disturbances in the brain that may cause abnormal muscle movements or unconsciousness.

symptoms—The body's signals that an illness or injury is present.

vaccine—A weakened form of a virus that causes the immune system to produce antibodies against that virus.

viral—Caused by a virus.

virus—A harmful particle that causes illnesses by invading an organism's cells in order to reproduce.

white blood cells—Immune system cells that identify and fight off antigens.

FIND OUT MORE

Organizations

Centers for Disease Control and Prevention
1600 Clifton Road
Atlanta, GA 30333
Phone: 1-800-CDC-INFO (232-4636)
www.cdc.gov/

National Institute of Allergy and Infectious Diseases (NIAID)
National Institutes of Health, DHHS
6610 Rockledge Drive, MSC 6612
Bethesda, MD 20892-6612
Phone: 1-866-284-4107
www3.niaid.nih.gov

Books

Diamond, Jared. *Guns, Germs, and Steel: The Fates of Human Societies*. New York: W. W. Norton, 2005.

Saffer, Barbara. *Measles and Rubella*. Chicago: Lucent Books, 2005.

Walker, Richard. *Epidemics and Plagues*. Boston: Houghton Mifflin Company, 2007.

Websites

BAM! Body and Mind
KidsHealth—Measles
http://kidshealth.org/parent/infections/bacterial_viral/
measles.html

Centers for Disease Control and Prevention—Body and Mind
www.bam.gov

U.S. National Library of Medicine—Mumps
www.nlm.nih.gov/medlineplus/mumps.html

INDEX

Page numbers for illustrations are in **boldface**.

ABOUT THE AUTHOR

L. H. Colligan writes about many topics, from health, science, and study skills to children's fiction. She gained her immunity to measles and mumps the hard way. Along with many class-mates in the 1950s, she caught both infections before vaccinations were available. Except for feeling miserable during both illnesses, she did not suffer any long-term effects.